KT-418-738

Sunderland

Andy Croft

NORWICH CITY COLLEGE LIBRARY

Stock No.	184165	
Class	796.334	
Cat.		Proc.	

Published in association with The Basic Skills Agency

Hodder & Stoughton

A MEMBER OF THE HODDER HEADLINE GROUP

184 165

Acknowledgements

Cover: David Davies/Allstar

Photos: pp 3, 6, 10, 14, 16, 20, 24 Popperfoto; p26 David Davies/Allstar

Every effort has been made to trace copyright holders of material reproduced in this book. Any rights not acknowledged will be acknowledged in subsequent printings if notice is given to the publisher.

Orders; please contact Bookpoint Ltd, 39 Milton Park, Abingdon, Oxon OX14 4TD. Telephone: (44) 01235 400414, Fax: (44) 01235 400454. Lines are open from 9.00–6.00, Monday to Saturday, with a 24 hour message answering service.
Email address: orders@bookpoint.co.uk

British Library Cataloguing in Publication Data
A catalogue record for this title is available from the British Library

ISBN 0 340 77667 6

First published 2000
Impression number   10 9 8 7 6 5 4 3 2 1
Year   2005 2004 2003 2002 2001 2000

Copyright © 2000 Andy Croft

All rights reserved. No part of this publication may be reproduced or transmitted in any form or by any means, electronic or mechanical, including photocopying, recording or any information storage and retrieval system, without permission in writing from the publisher or under licence from the Copyright Licensing Agency Limited. Further details of such licences (for reprographic reproduction) may be obtained from the Copyright Licensing Agency Limited, of 90 Tottenham Court Road, London W1P 9HE.

Typeset by GreenGate Publishing Services, Tonbridge, Kent.
Printed in Great Britain for Hodder and Stoughton Educational, a division of Hodder Headline Plc, 338 Euston Road, London NW1 3BH, by Redwood Books, Trowbridge, Wilts

Contents

1 The Black Cats

Sunderland are a very old club.
They are a very famous club.
They were once one of the biggest clubs
in England.

They have a famous history.
Champions six times.
Runners-up five times.
FA Cup finalists four times.
FA Cup winners twice.
Charity Shield winners twice.

They have a famous strip.
Red and white shirts and black shorts.
It is famous all over the world.
Miners from Sunderland once worked in Spain.
They took their team strip with them.
They gave it to a Spanish team
called Athletic Bilbao.
Athletic Bilbao still play in Sunderland's colours.

Their famous old ground was Roker Park.
World Cup games were played there in 1966.
Away teams hated playing at Roker Park.
The roar of the crowd was very loud.
It was called the Roker Roar.

Now Sunderland have a famous new ground.
The Stadium of Light is a beautiful stadium.
They play loud ballet music
when the teams come out
to scare the away team.
The Stadium of Light holds 42,000 people.
But it's too small for Sunderland supporters.
They are already building more seats!

Sunderland versus Aston Villa on September 9th, 1893.

They always get big crowds at Sunderland,
even when they lose.
But the fans know the losing days are over.

Sunderland are on their way back to the top.

2 Beginnings

Sunderland FC began a very long time ago,
back in 1879.
James Allan was a teacher in Sunderland.
He started a team.
They were all teachers.
They were called the Sunderland and District
Teachers Association Football Club.
They played in blue shirts and shorts.

The teachers did not earn very much.
After two years the club had no money.
One of the players sold his pet canary for £1.
It saved the club!

Sunderland Association Football Club 1895.

In 1887 Sunderland split.
There were lots of Scottish players in the team.
Some players thought there were too many.
They left to start another club
called Sunderland Albion.
But they soon went bust.

In the early years the club had
five different grounds.
In 1898 they moved to Roker Park.
That's why they were called the Rokermen.

3 The Team of All the Talents

In 1890 Sunderland joined the League.
They stayed in the top division
for the next 68 years.
Only Arsenal have stayed in longer than that.

Other teams did not want to play Sunderland.
They thought Sunderland was too far away!
So Sunderland had to pay their train fares.

Two years later Sunderland were Champions.
They had an amazing team.
With players like Johnny Campbell
and Tom Watson
They were called 'the Team of All the Talents'.
Ted Doig was their famous keeper.
He was called 'the Prince of Goalkeepers'.
He wore a cap strapped under his chin.
The forwards were Frank Cuggy,
Jackie Mordue and Charlie Buchan.
They were called 'the Sunderland Triangle'.

A painting of Ted Doig saving a goal.

Just look at their record:

1892 Champions
1893 Champions
1894 second
1895 Champions
1896 fifth
1898 second
1900 third
1901 second
1902 Champions

In 1913 Sunderland almost won the Double.
They were Champions for the fifth time.
But they lost 1–0 to Aston Villa
in the FA Cup Final.

4 The Bank of England

Roker Park used to hold 75,000 people.
It was always full.

Sunderland were a very rich club.
They were so rich they were called
'The Bank of England'.
They had some of the best players in Britain.

Dave Halliday scored 151 goals
in just four seasons.
He scored 43 goals one year.
Bobby Gurney scored 228 goals.
Charles Buchan scored 209 goals for the club.
Raich Carter scored 213 goals in 451 games.
Patsy Gallagher was called 'the mighty atom'.
He once did a somersault over the line
with the ball between his feet.

In 1935 Sunderland were second in the league.
In 1936 they won the Championship
for the sixth time
and beat Arsenal to win the Charity Shield.
In 1937 they reached the FA Cup Final again.
It was the first time a Cup Final was televised.
Preston scored first
but Sunderland won 3–1.

Sunderland captain Raich Carter holds the cup after their success in the 1937 Wembley Cup Final.

5 Decline

After the War
things went wrong for Sunderland.

They still had some great players,
like Billy Bingham, Stan Anderson
and Len Shackleton.
Shackleton was called
'the Clown Prince of Soccer'.
He had amazing ball control
and a good sense of humour.
He once scored six goals
against Newport County.
The final score was 13–0.
He said Newport were lucky to get nil!

Len Shackleton in action!

In 1958 Sunderland were relegated.
The fans could not believe it.

Brian Clough was Sunderland's best player.
He scored 53 goals in 58 games.
But it took six years to climb back
into the top flight.

They came back up in 1964.
Then they went down again.

6 Underdogs

In 1972–3 Sunderland were in
the Second Division.
They had a new manager called Bob Stokoe.
He took them back to winning ways.

They drew with Notts County in the FA Cup
and won the replay.
Then they drew with Reading
and won the replay.
Then they drew with Man City
and won the replay.
They beat Luton in the quarter-final.
They beat mighty Arsenal in the semi-final.

Sunderland were back at Wembley.
But they still had to play Leeds in the final.
Leeds were the best team in the land.
Everyone thought Leeds would win.
It was 40 years since a Second Division team
had won the Cup.

The Sunderland team that day
included legends like:
Dave Watson, Dennis Tuart,
Ian Porterfield and Bobby Kerr.
Legendary keeper Jim Montgomery
played 537 games for the club.

Bobby Kerr holds the cup high after their win against
Leeds United.

It was a hard match.
After thirty minutes
Ian Porterfield scored for Sunderland.
Leeds counter-atttacked.
Jim Montgomery was in goal.
In the seventieth minute he made
an amazing double save.
The final score was 1–0.
Sunderland had won the Cup!

At the end of the season Sunderland were promoted.

7 Up and Down

Sunderland only stayed up one season.
Then they went down again.

In 1980 they went back up.
That season they went down again.
They even slipped into the Third Division.

In 1990 they came back up.
The next season they went down again.

Sunderland fans were getting used to losing.

In 1985 they reached the League Cup Final
but they lost 1–0 to Norwich.

In 1992 they reached the FA Cup Final
but they lost 2–0 to Liverpool.

Were the glory days really over
for Sunderland?

8 The Stadium of Light

In 1995 Peter Reid became
Sunderland manager.
He used to play for England.
He took Sunderland back to the top.

In 1997 the club left Roker Park.
They moved to the Stadium of Light.

But that season they were relegated again.
The following season Kevin Phillips
scored 35 goals.
Sunderland reached the First Division play-offs.
But they lost in the final.

In 1999 they were First Division Champions.
Kevin Phillips was injured for four months.
But he still scored 25 goals.

Sunderland are now back in the Premiership.

The Stadium of Light, August 1997.

Peter Reid is a brilliant manager.
He has a brilliant stadium.
He has some amazing fans.
He has some great players:
Danny Dichio, Kevin Phillips,
Michael Gray, Stefan Schwarz,
Niall Quinn, Alex Rae,
Thomas Sorensen and Kevin Ball.

Sunderland celebrating after winning the First Division title in April 1999.

Will they stay up this time?
Can success return to Sunderland?

Whatever happens the fans will
always sing the Sunderland song:

Wise men say, only fools rush in,
But I can't help falling in love with you.
Sunderland! Sunderland!

If you have enjoyed reading this book, you may be interested in other titles in the *Livewire* series.

Middlesbrough
Nottingham Forest
Charlton Athletic
Wimbledon
Michael Owen
Alan Shearer
Tony Adams
Vinnie Jones
Ian Wright
Sheffield Wednesday
Derby County
Leeds United
Blackburn Rovers
West Ham United

Being a Striker
Being a Goalie
The World Cup